REVELATIONS
OF ST. BRIDGET

St. Bridget of Sweden

REVELATIONS
OF ST. BRIDGET

ON THE

LIFE AND PASSION
OF OUR LORD

AND THE

LIFE OF HIS BLESSED MOTHER

At the cross her station keeping,
Stood the mournful Mother weeping,
Close to Jesus to the last.
        —from the *Stabat Mater*

TAN BOOKS AND PUBLISHERS, INC.
Rockford, Illinois 61105

The *Revelations* of St. Bridget were examined by the learned divine, John de Torquemada, later a Cardinal, and approved as being doctrinally conformable to the true Faith.

This book of excerpts was translated from the 1611 Antwerp edition of the *Revelations* of St. Bridget. This book of excerpts was published by Academy Library Guild, Fresno, California; republished in 1965 by Apostolate of Christian Action, Fresno, California. Re-typeset and published in 1984 by TAN Books and Publishers, Inc.

Library of Congress Catalog Card No.: 83-51547

ISBN: 0-89555-233-7

Printed and bound in the United States of America.

TAN BOOKS AND PUBLISHERS, INC.
P.O. Box 424
Rockford, Illinois 61105

1984

CONTENTS

———•———

v

ABOUT ST. BRIDGET
OF SWEDEN

———•———

St. Bridget of Sweden, also known as St. Birgitta, was born in June of 1303 in Finsta, in the province of Uppland, Sweden. She was the fifth child of Birger Persson, a knight and governor, and Ingeborg Bengstdotter, both parents being just and devout and of noble lineage.

Mysterious prophecies attended Bridget's birth. Ingeborg narrowly escaped drowning not long before Bridget was born, and afterwards an angel appeared and told her she had been saved because of the child to be born to her. The angel added, "Bring her up in the love of God, for she is His gift to you."

As a child, Bridget did not speak until she was three years old, but when she did begin to speak it was more perfectly than is usual for children of that age. At age seven she saw her first heavenly vision: a beautiful lady offered her a precious crown; when Bridget accepted it, it was placed on her head so that she felt its touch. When she was ten years old she had another vision, a vision of Christ crucified, with blood flowing from His wounds.

Bridget was eleven years old when her mother died. She was then sent to live with her aunt, the Lady Katherine. When Bridget was thirteen years old, her father chose a husband for her—a young man of eighteen named Ulf, "rich, noble and wise." Bridget's heart had long since belonged to God, and looking back on this time years later, she said, "I would rather have died than marry!" Yet she accepted her father's choice as the will of God. She loved Ulf and lived her married life to the full.

At Bridget's request, she and Ulf lived in continence for one to two years, praying that if they came together carnally God would give them children who would serve Him and never displease Him. Bridget bore eight children, one of whom was to become St. Katherine of Sweden, also called St. Karin. St. Bridget brought her children up with great care; she was a gracious hostess to her many guests, and she practiced much penance and many works of charity—including tending the sick and reclaiming girls who had fallen into sin. She also spent six years as advisor and chief lady-in-waiting at the court of King Magnus II and Queen Blanche of Sweden and Norway.

When her husband died about the year 1343, St. Bridget increased her fasts and prayer vigils and dressed in poor garments—below those of her social rank. Her revelations became frequent. God made known to her that He had chosen her to be His bride and to give His warnings and messages to many people. He also revealed to her His will that she found the Religious Order of Our Most Holy Saviour (now commonly called the Bridgettines), which was to give a special honor to His Blessed Mother.

St. Bridget was told to go to Rome for the Holy Year of 1350. The Pope at that time was living in Avignon, France, and it was St. Bridget's mission—by pleading, prayer, and suffering—to try to bring him back to his rightful place at Rome.

Bridget lived in Rome for over twenty years. She performed many miracles. Her daughter Katherine joined her there, and together they worked among both rich and poor, showing to all an inexhaustible love. St. Bridget was remembered as homely and kind, and as having a smiling face. She died on July 23, 1373 and was canonized in 1391. The Pope declared her "Patron Saint of Sweden" in 1396.

PREFACE

———•———

To many of His saints, who meditated so devoutly and so affectionately on His Life and Passion, Our Blessed Lord has been pleased to exhibit them more clearly. Where supported by the recognized sanctity of the individual and the absence of delusion, the Church has permitted their circulation as useful and edifying, and many have in all ages had a certain weight with the faithful. It is not easy to explain what that weight is, except by saying that the use and influence of these revelations is purely devotional.

Among the revelations of canonized saints and other holy personages, none have exercised a wider influence, or been more frequently cited, than those of St. Bridget; and to make accessible to the English reader writings of which he has heard from childhood, we have selected from the old Latin folio such as bear on the Life and Passion of Our Lord and the life of His Blessed Mother, in the hope that they may increase the reader's love for both.

"Nothing is more famous in the life of St. Bridget," says the learned Alban Butler, "than the many revelations with which she was favored by God, chiefly concerning the sufferings of Our Blessed Saviour, and revolutions which were to happen in certain kingdoms. It is certain that God, who communicates Himself to His servants in many ways with infinite condescension, and distributes His gifts with infinite wisdom, treated this great saint and certain others with special marks of His goodness, conversing frequently with them in a most familiar manner, as the devout Blosius observes. Sometimes He spoke to them in visions, at other times He discovered to them hidden things by supernatural illustrations of their understandings, or by representations raised in their imaginations so clearly that they could not be mistaken in them; but to distinguish the operations of the Holy Ghost and the illusions of the enemy requires great prudence and attention to the just criteria or rules for the discernment of spirits. Nor can any private revelations ever be of the same nature, or have the same weight and certainty with those that are public, which were made to the prophets to be by them promulgated to the Church, and confirmed to men by the sanction of miracles and the authority of the Church.

"The learned divine, John de Torrecremata [Torquemada], afterwards Cardinal, by order of the Council of Basil [Basle], examined the book of St.

Bridget's revelations, and approved it as profitable
for the instruction of the faithful—which approbation was admitted by the Council as competent and
sufficient. However, it amounts to no more than a
declaration that the doctrine contained in that book
is conformable to the orthodox faith, and the revelations piously credible upon an historical probability.
The learned Cardinal Lambertini, afterwards Pope
Benedict XIV, writes upon this subject as follows:
'The approbation of such revelations is no more
than a permission that, after a mature examination,
they may be published for the profit of the faithful.
Though an assent of Catholic faith be not due to
them, they deserve a human assent according to the
rules of prudence, by which they are probable and
piously credible, as the revelations of Blessed
Hildegardis, St. Bridget, and St. Catherine of
Siena.' ''

The revelations of St. Bridget, as taken down by
her confessors, were printed as early as 1492, and
many subsequent editions have appeared. The
following translations are made from the Antwerp
edition of 1611, and are probably the first in English
of any part of her revelations, although the Angeli-
cal Discourse, or Office of Our Lady, was printed at
London, by Caxton, the first English printer.

CHAPTER I

Blessed art Thou, my Lord, my God, and most beloved lover of my soul, who art one God in three Persons. Glory and praise be to Thee, O my Lord Jesus Christ, who wast sent by Thy Father into the body of a Virgin, yet ever remainest with Thy Father in Heaven, the Father with His divinity remaining inseparably with Thee in Thy humanity in the world.

Honor and glory be to Thee, O my Lord Jesus Christ, who, conceived of the Holy Ghost in the Virgin's womb, didst corporally increase, and humbly dwell therein, to the time of Thy birth, and, after Thy joyful nativity, didst deign to be handled by Thy Mother's most pure hands, be wrapped in swaddling clothes, and laid in a manger.

Blessed art Thou, my Lord Jesus Christ, who didst

1

wish Thy immaculate flesh to be circumcised, and Thy name called Jesus, and also to be offered in the temple by Thy Mother.

Blessed art Thou, my Lord Jesus Christ, who caused Thyself to be baptized in the Jordan by Thy servant John.

Blessed be Thou, my Lord Jesus Christ, who didst preach with Thy blessed lips the words of life to men, and didst work many miracles personally before them.

Blessed be Thou, my Lord Jesus Christ, who, fulfilling the Scriptures of the prophets, didst reasonably show Thyself to the world to be true God.

Benediction and glory be to Thee, my Lord Jesus Christ, who didst wonderfully fast for forty days in the desert, and didst permit Thyself to be tempted by Thine enemy the devil, whom Thou didst drive off by a single word, when so it pleased Thee.

Blessed be Thou, my Lord Jesus Christ, who didst foretell Thy death before the time, and in the Last Supper didst wonderfully consecrate Thy precious Body of material bread, and also charitably gave it to Thy Apostles, in memory of Thy most worthy Passion, and by washing their feet with Thy sacred and precious hands, didst humbly show Thy very great humility.

Honor be to Thee, my Lord Jesus Christ, who through the fear of Thy Passion and death didst send forth blood from Thy body, and nevertheless didst perfect our redemption as Thou didst wish to do, and thus didst more manifestly show the charity which Thou didst bear the human race.

Glory be to Thee, my Lord Jesus Christ, who, sold by Thy disciple, and bought by the Jews, wast seized for us, and who didst cast Thy enemies to the ground by a single word, and didst afterwards, of Thy free will, give Thyself up a captive to their unclean, rapacious hands.

Blessed be Thou, my Lord Jesus Christ, who wast led to Caiphas, and who, though judge of all, didst humbly permit Thyself to be given up to the judgment of Pilate.

Blessed be Thou, my Lord Jesus Christ, who wast sent by Pilate the judge, to Herod, and didst suffer Thyself to be derided and despised by him, and didst consent to be sent back again to Pilate as judge.

Glory be to Thee, my Lord Jesus Christ, for the derision which Thou didst undergo, when, clothed in purple, Thou didst stand, crowned with most acute thorns; and, because Thou didst most patiently bear to be spit upon, in Thy glorious face, Thy eyes bound, and to be most violently beaten on the cheeks and neck by the malignant hands of the wicked.

Peace be to Thee, my Lord Jesus Christ, who didst most patiently suffer Thyself to be bound to a pillar, inhumanly scourged, led, streaming with blood, to Pilate's tribunal, and to be seen like an innocent lamb.

Blessed be Thou, my Lord Jesus Christ, who didst most patiently submit to hear, with Thy blessed ears, insults and lies vomited against Thee, and the voices of the people asking that a guilty robber should be absolved, and Thou, innocent, condemned.

Honor be to Thee, my Lord Jesus Christ, who, with Thy whole glorious body bathed in blood, wast condemned to die on the cross, and didst painfully bear Thy cross on Thy sacred shoulders, and wast furiously led to the place of Thy Passion and despoiled of Thy garments, and didst thus wish to be fastened to the cross.

Immense glory be to Thee, my Lord Jesus Christ, who didst humbly bear for us that the Jews should extend Thy venerable hands and feet with a rope, and cruelly fasten Thee to the wood of the cross with iron nails, and should call Thee a betrayer, and writing a title of confusion above Thee, should in manifold ways deride Thee with their horrid words.

Eternal praise and thanksgiving be to Thee, my Lord Jesus Christ, who didst so meekly endure such cruel pains for us; for when Thy blessed body lost all its strength on the cross, then Thy blessed eyes were darkened, Thy beautiful face, from loss of blood, was all overspread with pallor, Thy blessed tongue was parched and dried up, and Thy mouth was moistened by a most bitter draught. Thy hair and beard were filled with blood from the wounds of

Thy most sacred head. The bones of Thy hands and feet, and of all Thy precious body, were rent from their places, not without great and intense grief to Thee; the veins and nerves of all Thy blessed body were cruelly broken. And thus Thou wast inhumanly scourged and wounded with grievous wounds, that Thy most innocent skin and flesh were intolerably torn. And thus afflicted and tortured, Thou didst hang on the cross, O my most sweet Jesus, and in excessive pain didst patiently and humbly await the hour of death.

Perpetual honor be to Thee, my Lord Jesus Christ, who, in such agony, didst humbly look with benign eyes of charity on Thy most worthy Mother who never sinned, nor consented to even the slightest sin, and consoling her, didst faithfully commit her to the guardianship of Thy disciple.

Eternal benediction be to Thee, my Lord Jesus Christ, for each hour in which Thou didst endure the most intense bitterness and agony on the cross for us sinners. For the acute pain of Thy wounds keenly penetrated Thy happy soul, and cruelly pierced Thy most sacred heart, till, Thy heart breaking, Thou didst happily give up the ghost, and bowing down Thy head, didst humbly commend Thyself into the hands of God Thy Father, and then Thy dead body remained all cold.

Blessed be Thou, my Lord Jesus Christ, who for our salvation didst permit Thy side and heart to be pierced with a lance, and didst send forth copiously from the same side Thy precious blood and water to redeem us, and didst not wish Thy most sacred body to be taken down from the cross till permission was given by the judge.

Glory be to Thee, my Lord Jesus Christ, because Thou didst wish Thy blessed body to be taken down from the cross by Thy friends, and to be laid in the arms of Thy most afflicted Mother, and didst permit it to be wrapped by her in winding-sheets, and laid in the sepulcher, there to be guarded by soldiers.

Eternal honor be to Thee, my Lord Jesus Christ, who didst rise from the dead on the third day, and didst manifest Thyself alive to such as Thou didst wish, and after forty days, didst ascend in the sight of many to Heaven, and didst there honorably place Thy friends whom Thou hadst delivered from Limbo.

Eternal praise and jubilee be to Thee, my Lord Jesus Christ, who didst send down Thy Holy Spirit into the hearts of Thy disciples, and didst augment in their spirits immense divine love.

Blessed be Thou, and pleased and glorious forever, my Lord Jesus, who sittest on the throne in Thy kingdom of Heaven, in the glory of Thy divinity, living corporally with all Thy most holy members, which Thou didst assume of the flesh of a Virgin. And thus Thou wilt come on the day of judgment to judge the souls of all, living and dead.

Who livest and reignest with the Father and Holy Ghost, forever and ever.   Amen.

———•———

CHAPTER II

PRAYER OF PRAISE AND THANKSGIVING ON THE LIFE OF THE BLESSED VIRGIN

Blessed and venerated be thou, my Lady Virgin Mary, most holy Mother of God, whose noblest creature thou art, and who was never so closely loved as by thee, O glorious Lady.

Glory be to thee, my Lady Virgin Mary, Mother of God, who by the same angel by whom Christ was announced to thee, was announced to thy father and mother, and wast conceived and born in their most holy union.

Blessed be thou, my Lady Virgin Mary, who in thy most holy infancy, immediately after being weaned, wast borne by thy parents to God's temple, and committed, with other virgins, to the care of the devout high priest.

Praise be to thee, my Lady Virgin Mary, who when thou didst attain an age to know that God, thy Creator, existed, didst immediately begin to love

Him intensely, above all things, and didst then most discreetly order thy day and night in different offices and exercises to the honor of God, and didst so curtail the food and sleep of thy glorious body as to be apt to serve God.

Infinite glory be to thee, my Lady Virgin Mary, who didst humbly vow thy virginity to God, and therefore didst not care who espoused thee, because thou didst know that He to whom thou didst first pledge thy faith was more powerful and better than all.

Blessed be thou, my Lady Virgin Mary, who wast alone inflamed with the ardor of divine love, contemplating with all thy mind and with all the elevated virtue of thy powers, the most high God, to whom with ardent love thou hadst offered thy virginity, when the angel of God was sent to thee, and saluting thee, announced to thee the will of God. To whom, replying, thou didst most humbly declare thyself the handmaid of God, and the Holy Ghost wonderfully filled thee with all virtue. God the Father sent thee His coeternal and coequal Son, who, coming into thee, then assumed to Himself a human body of thy flesh and blood. And so, in that blessed hour, the Son of God became in thee thy Son, living with all His members, yet not losing His divine majesty.

Blessed be thou, my Lady Virgin Mary, who didst constantly feel the body of Christ, created by thy blessed body, grow and move in thy womb till the time of His glorious nativity. Whom thou before all others didst touch with thy sacred hands, wrap up in clothes, and, according to the oracle of the prophet, didst lay in a manger, and didst maternally nurture Him with the sacred milk of thy blessed breasts, in great joy of exultation.

Glory be to thee, O my Lady Virgin Mary, who, inhabiting a contemptible house—a stable—didst see powerful kings come from afar, to thy Son, humbly offering royal gifts with great reverence to thy Son. Whom afterwards thou didst present with thy precious hands in the Temple, and didst diligently lay up in thy blessed heart all things seen and heard in His infancy.

Blessed be thou, my Lady Virgin Mary, who didst fly to Egypt with thy most holy Son, whom thou didst afterwards bring with joy to Nazareth, and behold Him, thy Son, as He increased bodily, humble and obedient to thee and Joseph.

Blessed be thou, my Lady Virgin Mary, who didst behold thy Son preaching, working miracles, and choosing His Apostles, who, enlightened by His example, miracles, and doctrine, were made witnesses of the truth, announcing to all nations that thy Jesus was truly the Son of God, that it was He who had accomplished in Himself the oracles of the prophets, when He had patiently endured a most atrocious death for the human race.

Blessed be thou, my Lady Virgin Mary, who didst long beforehand know that thy Son was to be arrested, and didst afterwards, with thy blessed eyes, mournfully see Him bound and scourged, crowned with thorns, and fastened naked to the cross, and many despising Him and calling Him a seducer.

Honor be to thee, my Lady Virgin Mary, who didst painfully hear with thy blessed ears thy Son speaking to thee in pain from the cross, and crying to the Father in the agony of death, and commending His soul to His Father's hands.

Praise be to thee, my Lady Virgin Mary, who in bitter grief didst behold thy Son hanging on the cross, livid and stained with His own blood from the top of His head to the soles of His feet, and thus cruelly die; and didst most bitterly see His feet and hands, together with His glorious side, transpierced, and His whole skin torn without any mercy.

Blessed be thou, my Lady Virgin Mary, who with tearful eyes didst behold thy Son taken down, wrapped in winding-sheets, laid in the sepulcher, and there guarded by soldiers.

Blessed be thou, my Lady Virgin Mary, who didst depart from the sepulcher of thy Son with intense grief of thy deeply wounded heart, and wast borne, all full of grief, to John's house by thy friends, and didst there immediately feel a relief of thy great grief because thou didst most certainly foreknow that He would quickly rise again.

Rejoice, my most worthy Lady Virgin Mary, that the very moment thy Son rose from the dead, He wished this to be known to thee, His most blessed Mother, because He at once appeared in person to thee, then showed to others that He was risen from the dead, who underwent death in His living body.

Rejoice, then, my most worthy Lady Virgin Mary, who, death being conquered, and the agent of death supplanted and the way of Heaven laid open, didst see thy Son rising triumphant with the crown of victory, and on the fortieth day after His resurrection didst behold Him honorably ascend in the sight of many to His heavenly kingdom, attended like a king by angels.

Exult, my most worthy Lady Virgin Mary, that thou didst deserve to see how thy Son, after His ascension, sent down on His Apostles and disciples the Holy Ghost, wherewith He had already filled thee entirely, and increasing in them the fervor of charity and uprightness of Catholic faith, wonderfully enlightened their hearts.

Rejoice especially, my Lady Virgin Mary, and let the whole earth rejoice with thy joy, that thy Son permitted thee to remain many years in this world after His ascension, to console His friends and strengthen them in faith, to help the needy, and sagely counsel the Apostles.

And then, by thy most prudent words, most virtuous behavior, and holy deeds, He converted to the

Catholic faith innumerable Jews and pagan infidels, and wonderfully enlightened them to confess thee to be His Virgin Mother, and Himself thy Son, and God with a real humanity.

Blessed be thou, my Lady Virgin Mary, who from thy ardent charity and maternal love didst inceasingly, hour by hour, desire to go to thy beloved Son, now sitting in Heaven; and thou living in this world, by sighing for heavenly things, didst humbly conform thyself to the divine will, whereby, as divine justice dictated, thou didst unspeakably increase thy eternal glory.

Eternal honor and glory be to thee, my Lady Virgin Mary, who, when it pleased God to take thee from the exile of this world, and to honor thy soul eternally in His kingdom, vouchsafed to announce it to thee by His angel, and who wished thy venerable body, when dead, to be interred by the Apostles, with all reverence, in the sepulcher.

Rejoice, O my Lady Virgin Mary, that in thy calm death thy soul was embraced by the power of God, who paternally guarding it, protected it from all adversity. And then God the Father subjected all that is created to thy power; and the Son of God most honorably placed thee, His most worthy Mother, on a most exalted throne beside Him; and the Holy Ghost wonderfully exalted thee to His glorious kingdom, a Virgin espoused to Himself.

Rejoice eternally, my Lady Virgin Mary, that for

some days after thy death, thy body lay buried in the tomb, until, by the power of God, it was again honorably united to thy soul.

Exult, O Mother of God, glorious Lady Virgin Mary, that thou didst deserve to see thy body quickened after death, assumed with thy soul with angelic honors to Heaven, and didst see thy glorious Son, God with humanity, and with exulting joy behold Him to be the most just judge of all men, and the rewarder of good works.

Rejoice also, my Lady Virgin Mary, that the sacred flesh of thy body knew that it existed Virgin Mother in Heaven, and saw itself immaculate from all mortal and venial stain; nay, knew that thou hadst done all virtuous deeds so in love that it behooved God to honor thee with the highest honor. Then also didst thou understand that whosoever loves God more ardently in this world, will be placed nearer to Himself by God in Heaven. And as it was manifest to all the court of Heaven that no one, of angels or of men, loved God with as much charity as thou, therefore it was just and worthy that God Himself should honorably place thee, soul and body, on the highest seat of glory.

Blessed be thou, O my Lady Virgin Mary, that every faithful creature praises the Trinity for thee, because thou art His most worthy creature; who dost most promptly obtain pardon for wretched souls, and art the most faithful advocate and pleader for all sinners.

Praised then be God, supreme Emperor and Lord, who created thee to so great honor, that thou shouldst become perennially Empress and Lady in the kingdom of Heaven, to reign with Him eternally through ages of ages.   Amen.

———•———

CHAPTER III

THE IMMACULATE CONCEPTION

The Blessed Virgin Speaks

And it is a truth that I was conceived without original sin, and not in sin; because, as my Son and I never sinned, so no marriage was more holy than that from which I was born. *(Lib. vi, c. 49).*

A golden hour was my conception, for then began the principle of the salvation of all, and darkness hastened to light. God wished to do in His work something singular and hidden from the world, as He did in the dry rod blooming. But know that my conception was not known to all, because God wished that as the natural law and the voluntary election of good and bad preceded the written law, and the written law followed, restraining all inordinate notions, so it pleased God, that His friends should piously doubt of my conception, and that each should show his zeal till the truth became clear in its preordained time. *(Lib. vi, c. 55)*.

———•———

CHAPTER IV

BIRTH OF THE BLESSED VIRGIN

When I was born, it was not unknown to the demons, but speaking by a certain similitude, they thus thought: "So a certain virgin is born, what shall we do? For it is evident that something wonderful is to take place in her. If we throw around her all the nets of our malice, she will burst them like tow. If we examine all her heart, it is defended by a strong garrison. There is no spot in her for a spear to touch. Therefore, we may fear lest her purity be our torture. Her grace will crush all our strength; her constancy prostrate us beneath her feet." But the friends of God, who were in long expectation, said by divine inspiration: "Why grieve we more? We should rather rejoice, for the light is born that is to dispel our darkness, and our desire shall be accomplished." And the angels of God rejoiced, although their joy was always in the vision of God, saying: "Something desirable is born on earth, and especially beloved by God, whereby true peace shall be restored to Heaven and earth, and our losses shall be made up." Indeed, daughter, I assure thee, that my birth was the opening of true joy; for then came forth the rod from which that flower proceeded, whom kings and prophets desired. And when I had attained an age to know something of my Creator, then I turned to Him with unspeakable love, and desired Him with my whole heart. I was also preserved by wonderful grace, so that not even in my tender years did I consent to sin, because the love of God and my parents' care, good education, the preservation of good, and fervor of knowing God preserved with me. *(Lib. vi, c. 56).*

I am she, who from eternity have been in the love of God, and from my infancy the Holy Ghost was perfectly with me. And you may take an example from a nut, which, when it grows exteriorly, increases in the interior, so that the shell is always full, and there is no space to receive aught else. So I, from my childhood, was full of the Holy Ghost, and according to the increase of my body and age, the Holy Ghost filled me so copiously as to leave no room for the entrance of any sin. Hence I never committed a mortal or venial sin, for I was so ardent in the love of God, that nothing was pleasing to me except the perfect will of God; for the fire of divine love was enkindled in my soul, and God, blessed above all, who created me by His power, and filled me with the virtue of the Holy Ghost, had an ardent love for me. *(Lib. iii, c. 8)*.

———•———

CHAPTER V

EARLY LIFE OF THE BLESSED VIRGIN

As soon as I understood that there was a God, I was always solicitous and fearful for my salvation and observance. And when I heard more fully that God was, too, my Creator, and judge of all my actions, I loved Him intensely, and every hour feared and pondered lest I should offend Him in word or deed. Then when I heard that He had given a law to His people, and His commandments, and wrought so many wonders with them, I firmly resolved in my mind to love naught but Him, and all worldly things became most bitter to me. Hearing after this that this same God was to redeem the world and be born of a virgin, I was filled with such love for her, that I thought of naught but God, wished naught but Him. I withdrew as much as possible from the converse and presence of kindred and friends. All that I could have I gave to the poor, reserving to myself only scanty food and clothing. Nothing pleased me but God. Ever did I long in my heart to live to the time of His birth, if perchance I might be worthy to be the unworthy handmaid of the mother of God. I also vowed in my heart to observe virginity if it was pleasing to Him, and to possess nothing in the world. But if God willed otherwise, that His will, not mine, be done; because I believed Him omnipotent, and desirous of naught but my good, so that I committed my will absolutely to Him.

As the time approached, when by rule, virgins were presented in the Temple of the Lord, I went up among them in submission to my parents, thinking that nothing was impossible to God. And as He knew that I desired nothing, wished nothing but Himself, He could, if it pleased Him, preserve me in my virginity; if not, His will be done. After hearing all the instructions in the Temple, I returned home, inflamed with still greater love of God, enkindled daily by new fervor and desire of love. I accordingly retired apart from all more than usual, and I was alone night and day fearing most intensely lest tongue should speak or ear hear aught against my God, or eyes see aught delightful. Even in my silence was I timid and most anxious, lest I should be silent when I ought rather to speak. When I was thus troubled in heart alone by myself, and committed all my hope to God, at once it came into my mind to think of God's great power, how the angels and all things created serve Him, and what was His glory, which is ineffable and interminable. For I saw the sun, but not as it shines in Heaven; I saw light, but not such light as shines in the world. I perceived an odor, not like that of plants or anything of the kind, but most sweet and almost ineffable with which I was all filled, and exulted for joy. Then immediately I heard a voice, but from no human lips. And on hearing it I feared considerably, thinking within myself whether it was an illusion, and forthwith an angel of God appeared before me, like a most beautiful man, but not clothed in flesh, who said to me: "Hail, Mary, etc." When I heard this, I wondered what this meant, or why he uttered such a salutation; for I knew myself, and deemed myself unworthy of this or of any good. But it is not impossible to God to do whatsoever He willeth. Then the angel said again: "What is born in thee is holy, and shall be called the Son of God; and as it shall please Him, so shall it be done." Still I deemed myself unworthy, and asked the angel not why or when, but how it should be done, that I, unworthy, should be the Mother of God, not knowing man. And the angel answered me as I said: "Nothing is impossible to God, but whatsoever He willeth shall come to pass, etc." Hearing the words of the angel, I felt a most fervent desire to be the Mother of God, and my soul spoke in love: "Here I am, let Thy will be done in me." At this word my Son was instantly conceived in my womb, with unspeakable exultation of my soul and my whole body. And when I had Him in my womb, I bore Him without pain, without any weight or feeling of inconvenience. In all things I humbled myself, knowing that He was almighty whom I bore. And when I brought Him forth, I brought Him forth without pain and sin, as I conceived Him, with such exultation of soul and body, that for exultation my feet did not feel the ground they stood upon. And as He entered all my members with the joy of my whole soul, so with the joy of my whole body, my soul exulting with ineffable joy, He came forth, my virginity untouched. And when I beheld Him and considered His beauty, my soul in joy distilled, as it were, dew, knowing myself unworthy of such a Son. But when I considered the places of the nails in His hands and feet, which according to the prophets, I heard were to be crucified, then my eyes filled with tears and my heart was breaking with sadness. And when my Son gazed into my streaming eyes, He was sorrowful unto death. But when I considered the power of His deity, I was again consoled, knowing that He so willed it, and that so it was expedient, and I conformed my will to His will, and thus my joy was tempered by pain.

CHAPTER VI

THE VISITATION

When the angel announced to me that I should bear a Son, as soon as I consented, I felt something amazing and inexplicable in me, so that greatly wondering, I at once went up to my cousin Elizabeth to console her in her pregnancy and confer with her on what the angel had announced to me. And when she met me at the well, and we enjoyed each other's embrace and kiss, the infant in her womb, by a wonderful and visible motion, rejoiced. And I likewise was then moved in my heart by unwonted exultation, so that my tongue spoke unpremeditated words of God, and my soul could scarce contain itself for joy. And when Elizabeth wondered at the fervor of spirit that spoke in me, and I not otherwise wondered at the grace of God in her, we remained together many days blessing God. And after this a certain thought began to impress my mind, how and how devoutly I should act after so great a favor bestowed on me. What should I reply, if asked how I conceived, or who was the father of the Son I was to bear; or lest perchance Joseph, instigated by the enemy, should suspect me of evil. While thinking of these things, an angel, not unlike the one whom I had seen before, stood by me, saying: "Our God, who is eternal, is with thee and in thee. Fear not then, He will give thee to speak, He will direct thy steps and abode. He will perfect His work with thee powerfully and wisely.'' But Joseph, to whom I had been confided, when he perceived me to be pregnant, wondering and thinking himself unworthy to dwell with me, was troubled, not knowing what to do, till the angel told him in sleep: "Depart not from the virgin confided to thee, for it is most true as thou hast heard from her; for she has conceived of the Spirit of God, and shall bear a Son, the Saviour of the world. Therefore, serve her faithfully, and be thou the guardian and witness of her purity.'' Then from that day Joseph served me as his lady, and I humbled myself to his lowest labor. After this I was constantly in prayer, rarely wishing to see or be seen, and most rarely going forth, unless to the appointed feasts; and I was assiduous in the watches and readings given by our priests. I had a fixed time for manual labor, and I was discreet in fasting as much as my constitution could bear in God's service. Whatever we had over our daily sustenance we gave to the poor, content with what we had. Joseph so served me, that no scurrilous, murmuring, or angry word was heard from him, for he was most patient in poverty, solicitous in labor when it was necessary, most mild to those who reproached, most obedient in my service, a most prompt defender against those who gainsaid my virginity, a most faithful witness of the wonders of God. For he was so dead to the world

and the flesh that he never desired aught but
heavenly things. And so confident was he in God's
promises, that he would constantly exclaim: "Would
that I could live to see God's will fulfilled!" Most
rarely did he go to gatherings of men and their
councils, because his whole desire was to obey the
will of God, and therefore is his glory now so great.
(Lib. vi, c. 59).

———◆———

CHAPTER VII

HER LIFE WITH ST. JOSEPH

The Blessed Virgin Speaks

Know most certainly that before he married me,
Joseph knew in the Holy Ghost, that I had vowed my
virginity to my God, and was immaculate in
thought, word, and deed, and that he espoused me
with the intention of serving me, holding me in the
light of a sovereign mistress, not a wife. And I knew
most certainly in the Holy Ghost that my perpetual
virginity would remain intact, although by a secret
dispensation of God I was married to a husband. But
when I had consented to the annunciation of God,

Joseph, seeing my womb increase by the operation of the Holy Ghost, feared vehemently: not suspecting anything amiss in me, but remembering the sayings of the prophets, foretelling that the Son of God should be born of a virgin, deeming himself unworthy to serve such a mother, until the angel in a dream ordered him not to fear, but to minister unto me in charity.

Of worldly things Joseph and I reserved naught to ourselves, except the necessaries of life for the honor of God, distributing the rest for the love of God.

When the time of my Son's nativity approached, I came according to the foreknowledge of God to Bethlehem, bringing a most clean dress and clothes for my Son, which no one had ever used. In these I first wrapped Him who was born of me in all purity, and although from all eternity I was ordained to sit on the highest throne and honor, yet in my humility, I did not disdain to prepare and minister what was necessary for Joseph and myself. *(Lib. vii, c. 35).*

CHAPTER VIII

THE NATIVITY

When I was at the crib of Bethlehem, I beheld a
most beautiful Virgin with child, in a white mantle
and tunic, evidently soon about to be delivered.
With her was a most venerable old man, and they
had an ox and an ass. When they entered the cave,
the old man tied the ox and the ass to the crib; going
out he brought the Virgin a lighted torch, and set it
in the wall. Then he again withdrew so as not to be
personally present at the birth. Then the Virgin
loosed her shoes from off her feet, and laid aside her
white mantle, and took off her veil from her head,
and laid it beside her, remaining in her tunic, her
long hair, as beautiful as gold, falling down over her
shoulders. Then she drew out two fine, clean linen
cloths, and two of wool, which she had brought to
wrap the new-born Child in, and two smaller linen
ones to cover and tie His head. These she laid beside
her to use in due time. When all these things were
ready, then the Virgin, kneeling with great
reverence, placed herself in prayer, with her back to
the crib, her face eastward, raised to Heaven. She
stood with uplifted hands, and eyes fixed on Heaven,
rapt as it were, in an ecstasy of contemplation, in-
ebriated with the divine sweetness. And while she
thus stood in prayer, I beheld her Child move in her

womb, and at once in a moment, and in the twinkling of an eye, she brought forth her Son, from whom such ineffable light and splendor radiated, that the sun could not be compared to it; nor did the torch which the old man had set, in any manner give light, because that divine splendor had totally annihilated the material splendor of the torch, and so sudden and momentary was that mode of bearing, that I could not perceive or discern how, or in what part she brought forth. Nevertheless, I immediately beheld that glorious Babe lying naked and most pure on the ground, His flesh most clean from all filth or impurity. . . . I then also heard angelic chants of wonderful suavity and great sweetness. . . . When the Virgin perceived that she had been delivered, she immediately bowed her head, and joining her hands, adored her Son with great respect and reverence, saying: "Welcome, my God, and my Lord, and my Son." Then the Child crying, and, as it were, shivering with cold and the hard floor where He lay, turned a little, and stretched out His limbs, seeking to find a mother's favor and caress. Then His mother took Him in her hands and clasped Him to her heart, and with her cheek and breast warmed Him with great joy, and a mother's tender compassion. Then sitting on the ground, she laid her Son in her lap . . . and began diligently to wrap Him up, at first in linen and then in woolen cloths, and drawing them tight on His little body, bound His legs and arms with fillets tied to the four corners of the outer woolen cloth. And then she wrapped on her Son's head the two small linen cloths, which she had ready for the purpose. When this was done, the old man entered, and prostrating himself on his knees on the ground, he adored Him, weeping for joy. Nor did the Virgin on this occasion lose color or strength, as befalls other women who are delivered, except that her size was diminished. Then she arose with the Child in her arms, and both together, that is, she and Joseph, laid Him in the manger, and kneeling, adored Him with immense joy and gladness. *(Lib. vii, c. 21).*

While the Blessed Virgin and Joseph were adoring the Infant in the crib, I beheld the shepherds, and those that tended the flocks, come to see and adore the Child. When they saw Him, they immediately adored Him with great reverence and joy; and afterwards returned, praising and glorifying God for all that they had heard and seen. *(Lib. vii, c. 23).*

The Blessed Virgin Speaks

My daughter, know that I bore my Son as you have seen, praying alone on my knees in the stable. I bore Him with such joy and exultation of mind that I felt no pain or difficulty when He left my body. But I immediately wrapped Him up in clean swaddling clothes which I had previously prepared. When Joseph saw this, he wondered with great joy that I had been delivered without any aid; but as the great multitude of people in Bethlehem was busy with the census, the wonders of God could not be divulged among them. And therefore, know truly, that although men, according to human ideas, would assert that my Son was born in the usual way, it is true beyond all doubt that He was born as I tell thee and thou hast seen. *(Lib. vii, c. 23)*.

Daughter, know that when the three royal Magi came into the stable to adore my Son, I knew of their coming by prescience. And when they entered and adored Him, then my Son exulted, and for joy wore a more cheerful countenance. I, too, rejoiced and exulted in wonderful joy of mind, observing their words and actions, retaining them and laying them up in my heart. *(Lib. vii, c. 24)*.

———•———

CHAPTER IX

THE PURIFICATION

I did not need purification, like other women, because my Son who was born of me made me clean. Nor did I contract the least stain, who bore my most pure Son without any stain. Nevertheless, that the law and the prophecies might be fulfilled, I chose to live according to the law. Nor did I live like worldly parents, but humbly conversed with the humble. Nor did I wish to show anything extraordinary in me, but loved whatever was humble. On that day as today was my pain increased. For though, by divine inspiration, I knew that my Son was to suffer, yet this grief pierced my heart more keenly at Simeon's words, when he said that a sword should pierce my soul, and that my Son should be set for a sign to be contradicted. And until I was assumed in body and soul to Heaven, this grief never left my heart, although it was tempered by the consolation of the spirit of God. I also wish you to know that from that day my grief was sixfold. The first was in my knowledge: for every time that I looked upon my Son, wrapped Him in His swaddling clothes, or gazed upon His hands and feet, so often was my soul swallowed up, as it were, by fresh grief, for I thought how He was to be crucified. In the second place, there was pain in my hearing: for as often as I heard the opprobriums heaped on my Son, the falsehoods uttered against Him, the snares laid for Him, my soul was so afflicted that I could scarcely contain myself; but by the power of God, my grief knew bounds and respect, so that no impatience or levity was seen in me. In the third place, I suffered by sight: for when I beheld my Son bound and scourged, and suspended on the cross, I fell, as it were, lifeless; but recovering myself, I stood mourning and suffering so patiently, that neither my enemies nor any others beheld anything but gravity in me. My fourth suffering was in the touch: for I with others took my Son down from the cross, wrapped Him up, and laid Him in the tomb; and thus my grief increased, so that my hands and feet had scarce strength to bear me. Oh, how gladly would I then have been laid beside my Son! Fifthly, I suffered by a vehement desire of joining my Son after He ascended to Heaven, because the long delay which I had in this world, after His Ascension, increased my grief. Sixthly, I suffered from the tribulations of the Apostles and friends of God, ever fearing and grieving: fearing that they might yield to temptations and tribulations, grieving because my Son's words were everywhere contradicted. But though the grace of God always persevered with me, and my will always conformed to the will of God, yet my grief was constantly mingled with consolation, till I was assumed, body and soul, to my Son in Heaven. Let not, then, this grief leave thy heart, for without tribulation few would reach Heaven. (*Lib. vi, c. 57*).

CHAPTER X

ON THE FLIGHT INTO EGYPT

Jesus saith: Why did I flee into Egypt? I answer: Before the fall, there was one way to Heaven, broad and clear: broad in the abundance of virtues, clear in the divine wisdom and the obedience of a good will. Then the will being changed, there were two ways, one leading to Heaven, the other from it; obedience led to Heaven, disobedience seduced. [Thus there was a] choice of good and evil, obedience and disobedience, because he wished otherwise than God wished him to wish. To save man, it was right and just that one should come who might redeem him, and be possessed of perfect obedience and charity, and in whom those who wished might show charity, and those who wished, malice. But no angel could be sent to redeem man, because I, God, gave not My glory to another, nor was a man found who could appease Me for himself, still less for others. Hence I, sole just God, came to justify all.

By My flight to Egypt, I showed the infirmities of My humanity, and fulfilled the prophecies; I gave, too, an example to My disciples, that sometimes persecution is to be avoided for the greater future glory of God. That I was not found by My pursuers, the counsel of My Deity prevailed over man's counsel, for it is not easy to fight against God. That the innocents were slain was a sign of My future Passion, a mystery of those to be called, and of divine charity; for though the innocents did not bear testimony unto Me by voice and mouth, yet they did by their death, as agreed with My childhood; because it was foreseen that even in the blood of innocents, praise should be perfected to God. For though the malice of the unjust unjustly afflicted them, yet My divine permission, ever just and benignant, exposed them only justly, to show the malice of men and the incomprehensible counsel and piety of My divinity. Therefore, when unjust malice wreaked itself on the children, there justly superabounded merit and grace; and where the confession of the tongue and age were wanting, there the blood shed accumulated the most perfect good. *(Lib. v, inter. xii, sol. 4).*

———•———

CHAPTER XI

THE LIFE OF JESUS BEFORE HIS PASSION

Mary speaketh: I have spoken to thee of my dolors; but that dolor was not the least which I experienced when I bore my Son in my flight to Egypt, and when I heard the innocents slaughtered, and

Herod pursuing my Son. But although I knew what was written of my Son, yet my heart, for the excessive love I bore my Son, was filled with grief and sadness. You may perhaps ask what my Son did all that time of His life before His Passion. I reply that, as the Gospel says, He was subject to His parents, and He acted like other children till He reached His majority. Nor were wonders wanting in His youth: how idols were silenced, and fell in numbers in Egypt at His coming; how the Wise Men foretold that my Son should be a sign of great things to come; how, too, the ministries of angels appeared; how, too, no uncleanness appeared upon Him, nor entanglement in His hair, all which it is unnecessary for thee to know, as signs of His divinity and humanity are set forth in the Gospel, which may edify thee and others. But when He came to more advanced years, He was in constant prayer, and obediently went up with us to Jerusalem and elsewhere to the appointed feasts; so wonderful then were His sight and words, and so acceptable, that many in affliction said: "Let us go to Mary's Son, by whom we may be consoled." But increasing in age and wisdom, wherewith He was replete from the first, He labored with His hands in such things as were becoming, and spoke to us separately words of consolation and divinity, so that we were continually filled with unspeakable joy. But when we were in fear, poverty, and difficulty, He did not make for us

gold and silver, but exhorted us to patience, and we
were wonderfully preserved from the envious. Necessaries were occasionally furnished to us by the
compassion of pious souls, sometimes from our own
labor, so that we had what was necessary for our ac-
tual support, but not for superfluity, for we only
sought to serve God. After this, He conversed
familiarly with friends who came to the house, on
the law, and its meanings and figures; He also
openly disputed with the learned, so that they wondered, saying: "Ho! Joseph's Son teaches the
masters; some great spirit speaketh in Him." Once
as I was thinking of His Passion, seeing my sadness,
He said: "Dost thou not believe, Mother, that I am
in the Father, and the Father in Me? Wast thou
sullied when I entered thee, or in pain when I came
forth? Why art thou contracted by sadness? For it is
the will of My Father that I suffer death; nay, My
will with the Father. What I have of the Father cannot suffer; but the flesh which I took of thee shall
suffer, that the flesh of others may be redeemed, and
their spirits saved." He was so obedient that when
Joseph by chance said: Do this or that, He immediately did it, because He so concealed the power
of His divinity that it could not be discerned except
by me, and sometimes by Joseph, who both often
saw an admirable light poured around Him, and
heard angelic voices singing over Him. We also saw
that unclean spirits, which could not be expelled by

tried exorcists in our law, departed at the sight of my Son's presence.

———•———

CHAPTER XII

OUR LORD'S APPEARANCE

Such as my Son is in Heaven you cannot behold. But hear what He was in body in the world. He was so beautiful of countenance that no one looked Him in the face without being consoled by His aspect, even if heartbroken with grief. The just were consoled with spiritual consolation; and even the bad were relieved from worldly sadness as long as they gazed upon Him. Hence, those in grief were wont to say: "Let us go and see Mary's Son; we shall be relieved for that time."

In His twentieth year He was perfect in manly strength and stature. Amid those of modern times He would be large, not fleshy, but of large frame and muscle. His hair, eyebrows, and beard were of a light brown, His beard a hand's width long. His forehead not prominent or retreating, but erect. His nose moderate, neither small nor large; His eyes were so pure that even His enemies delighted to look upon Him; His lips not thick, but clear red. His chin was not prominent or over long, but graceful in beautiful moderation. His cheeks modestly fleshy, His complexion clear white and red. His bearing erect, and His whole body spotless. *(Lib. iv, c. 70).*

———•———

CHAPTER XIII

THE BAPTISM OF OUR LORD IN THE JORDAN

Jesus speaketh: Why did I choose to be baptized? Whoever wishes to found or begin a new way must necessarily, as the founder or beginner of the new way, precede others. Hence to the ancient people was given a certain carnal way, circumcision, in sign of future obedience and purgation, which in faithful and law-keeping persons, before I, the Son of God, the promised Truth, came, operated a certain effect of future grace and promise; and when the Truth came, as the law was only a shadow, it was decreed in eternity that the ancient way should depart, being now ineffectual. When, then, the Truth appeared and the shadow departed, and an easier way to Heaven was shown, I, God and man, born without sin, chose to be baptized from humility, and as an example to others, and to open Heaven to believers. And as a sign of this, when I was baptized, then Heaven opened, and the voice of My Father was heard, and the Holy Ghost appeared in the form of a dove, and I, the Son of God, was manifest in true man, that the faithful might know and believe that the Father opened Heaven to the faithful baptized, the Holy Ghost is with the baptizer, and the power of My humanity in the element, although the operation and will of the Father, Myself, and the Holy Ghost are but one. So when Truth came, that is, when I came into the world, then immediately the shadow disappeared, the shell of the law was broken, and the kernel appeared, circumcision ceased, and baptism was confirmed in Myself, whereby Heaven is opened to young and old, and children of wrath become children of grace and eternal life. *(Lib. v, inter. x, sol. 6).*

CHAPTER XIV

THE STATE OF THE WORLD WHEN CHRIST
BEGAN TO PREACH

The Son of God said: Before My Incarnation this world was like a wilderness, in which was a turbid and unclean well, of which all who drank, thirsted the more, and the sore-eyed became more afflicted. By this well stood two men, one of whom, crying out, said: "Drink securely, because the physician comes to take away all langor." The other said: "Drink in joy; it is vain to long for the uncertain." Moreover, seven roads led to the well, and therefore all desired it. Much doth the world resemble a desert, with wild beasts, fruitless trees, and unclean waters; because man, like a wild beast, was eager to pour out his neighbor's blood, unfruitful in works of justice, and unclean by incontinence and cupidity. In this wilderness, then, men sought the turbid well—that is, the love of the world and its honor, which is high in pride, turbid in the care and solicitude of the flesh—and by the seven mortal sins had, as it were, entrance by seven ways.

The two men standing by the well signified the masters of the Jews and Gentiles. For the doctors of the Jews were proud of the law which they had and did not keep, and as they were full of avarice they incited the people by word and example to seek temporal things, saying: "Live securely, for the Messias will come and restore all things." And the doctors of the Gentiles said: "Use the creatures that you see, for the world was made for us to enjoy." And when man stood so blind as to think neither of God nor hereafter, then I, God with the Father and Holy Ghost, came into the world, and assuming humanity, said openly: "What God promised and Moses wrote, is fulfilled. Love, therefore, the things of Heaven, for those of earth pass, and those of eternity will I give unto you." I showed, too, the sevenfold way whereby man might be drawn away from his vanity. For I showed poverty and obedience, I taught fasts and prayers; I sometimes fled away from men, and abode alone in prayer; I endured opprobrium, I chose toil and grief, I bore pain and contempt. In My Own Self did I show the way, in which My friends long walked, but now the way is broken up. The guardians sleep, those who pass delight in vanity and novelties; therefore, I rise and will not be silent. I will take away the voice of praise, and I will let My vineyard to others, who will bear fruit in season. Yet, according to the common proverb, friends are found among enemies. Therefore will I send to My friends words sweeter than dates, more delicious than honey, more precious than gold. Who receive and keep them shall have that treasure which is happily forever, and faileth not, but increases in life everlasting.

Before I began to walk and labor, a voice resounded before Me, saying: "The axe is laid to the tree." What was this voice but John the Baptist, who, sent before Me, cried out in the desert: "The axe is laid to the tree," as if to say: "Man is now ready, because the axe is ready." And he came, preparing the way to the city, and extirpating all obstacles. And I, coming, labored from sunrise to sunset, that is, from My Incarnation to My death on the cross; I worked out man's salvation, flying in the beginning of My entrance into this wilderness, on account of the persecution of Herod, My enemy; and I suffered persecution, I ate and drank, and fulfilled all the other necessities of nature, without sin, to the instruction of faith and the manifestation of My true assumed nature. *(Lib. iii, c. 15)*.

———•———

CHAPTER XV

THE AGONY IN THE GARDEN

Jesus speaks: I had three things in My death. First, Faith, when I bent My knees and prayed, knowing that the Father could deliver Me from My Passion. Second, Hope, when I waited so constantly and said:

"Not as I will." Third, Charity, when I said: "Thy will be done." I had, too, anguish of body and the natural fear of My Passion, when the blood issued from My body. Let not My friends then tremble as if abandoned when tribulation comes upon them; I showed them in Myself that weak flesh always shrinks from trouble. But you may ask: How did a bloody sweat issue from My body? As the blood of the sick man is dried and consumed in all his members, so My blood was consumed by the natural fear of death. Finally, My Father wishing to show the way by which Heaven should be opened and excluded man enter in, out of love delivered Me up to the Passion, that by accomplishing it, My body might be glorified. For in justice, My humanity could not enter glory without passion, although I might have done so by the power of My divinity.

How then do they deserve to enter into My glory who have little faith, vain hope, and no charity? If, indeed, they had the faith of eternal joy and horrible punishment, they would desire naught but Me. Did they believe that I know and see all things, and am powerful over all things, and seek judgment of all, the earth would grow vile to them, and they would be more afraid of sin before Me for fear of Me, than before men. Had they firm hope, then their whole mind and thought would be to Me. Had they divine charity, they would at least think in mind what I did for them, how great was My labor in preaching, My pain in My Passion, My charity in death, because I preferred death to abandoning them. But their faith is weak, tottering, as it were, to fall; because they believe, when the assault of temptation is absent—they distrust, when anything contrary comes upon them. Their hope is vain; they hope that sin will be forgiven without justice and truth of judgment. They trust to obtain the kingdom of Heaven gratis; they desire to obtain mercy untempered by justice. Their love towards Me is all cold, because they are never inflamed to seek Me unless compelled by tribulation. How can I be warm with such, who have neither right faith, firm hope, nor fervent love for Me? So when they cry out to Me and say: "Have mercy on me, O God," they do not deserve to be heard, nor to enter into My glory. As they will not follow their Lord to His Passion, they shall not follow Him to His glory. For no soldier can please his lord, and, after falling, be restored to favor, unless he first humbles him to show his contempt. *(Lib. i, c. 39).*

CHAPTER XVI

THE PASSION OF OUR LORD

The Blessed Virgin Speaks

At that time, my Son was suffering, and as Judas the traitor approached, He stooped towards him—for Judas was of low stature—giving him a kiss, saying: "Friend, wherefore hast thou come?" And immediately some seized Him, others dragged Him by the hair, others defiled Him by spitting upon Him. Then my Son spoke, saying: "I am reputed as a worm, which lies in winter as if dead, on which the passer-by spits and tramples. The Jews have this day treated Me like a worm, because I was deemed most abject and unworthy by them." *(Lib. iv, c. 99)*.

When the time of my Son's Passion arrived, His enemies seized Him, striking Him on His cheek and neck; and spitting upon Him, they mocked Him. Then, led to the pillar, He stripped Himself, and Himself stretched His hands to the pillar, which His enemies, pitiless, bound. Now, while tied there He had no clothing, but stood as He was born, and suffered the shame of His nakedness. Then His enemies rose up, for they stood on all sides, His friends having fled, and they scourged His body, pure from all spot or sin. At the first blow, I, who stood nearest, fell as if dead, and on recovering my

senses I beheld His body bruised and beaten to the
very ribs, so that His ribs could be seen; and what
was still more bitter, when the scourge was raised,
His very flesh was furrowed by the thongs. And
when my Son stood thus, all bloody, all torn, so that
no soundness could be found in Him nor any spot to
scourge, then one, his spirit roused within him,
asked: "Will you slay Him thus unjudged?" and he
immediately cut His bonds. Then my Son put on
His clothes, and I beheld the spot where my Son's
feet stood all full of blood, and I knew my Son's
course by His footprints, for wherever He went, the
earth seemed stained with blood; nor did they suffer
Him to clothe Himself, but they compelled and
urged Him to hasten.

Now, as my Son was led away like a robber, He
wiped away the blood from His eyes. And when He
was condemned, they gave Him His cross to bear.
When He had carried it a short way, one came up
and assumed it. Meanwhile, as my Son was going to
the place of His Passion, some smote Him on the
back, others struck Him in the face. And so violently
and rudely was He struck that though I did not see
the person striking, I distinctly heard the sound of
the blow. And when I came with Him to the place of
the Passion, I there beheld all the instruments prepared for His death. And my Son Himself, coming
thither, divested Himself of His clothes, the atten-
dants saying to each other: "These vestments are

ours, nor can He have them again, that is condemned to death.'' Now, while my Son stood as naked as when He was born, one, running up, handed Him a cloth with which, exulting inwardly, he covered Him. Then His cruel executioners seized Him, and stretched Him on the cross. First they fixed His right hand to the beam, which was pierced for nails, and they transfixed His hand in the part where the bone was firmest. Then drawing His other hand with a rope, they affixed it in like manner to the cross. Then they crucified His right foot, and over it the left, with two nails, so that all the nerves and veins were extended and broken. This done, they fitted a crown of thorns to His head, which so acutely wounded the venerable head of my Son that His eyes were filled, His ears stopped up, with the blood that streamed down, and His whole beard matted with the gore. And as He stood thus pierced and bloody, condoling with me as I stood mourning, He looked with blood-stained eyes to John, my kinsman, and commended me to him. At that time I heard some saying that my Son was a robber, others that He was a liar, others that none better deserved death than my Son, and these words renewed my grief. But, as has been said, when the first nail was driven into Him, horrified at the first blow, I fell as though dead, my eyes darkened, my hands trembling, my feet quivering, nor for bitterness could I look again before He was nailed fast.

On rising, I beheld my Son hanging miserably, and I, His most wretched mother, filled with terror on all sides, could scarcely stand for grief. But my Son, seeing me and His friends weeping disconsolately, in a loud and tearful voice cried out to His Father, saying: "Father, why hast Thou forsaken Me?" Then His eyes appeared half dead, His cheeks hollow, and His countenance mournful, His mouth open and His tongue bloodstained, His body collapsed as though He had nothing within, the humors being all drained, and His whole body pale and languid from the loss and flow of blood. His hands and feet were stretched out most rigidly, drawn and shaped to the form of the cross, His beard and hair all clotted with blood. Now when my Son was thus torn and livid, His heart alone was vigorous, it being naturally very good and strong; for at His birth He assumed a most pure body of my flesh, and an excellent constitution. His skin was so tender and fair that it could not be slightly struck without blood issuing at once. His blood was so fresh that it could be seen in His clear skin; and as He was of an excellent temperament, life struggled with death in His pierced body. For sometimes the pain mounted from His pierced limbs and nerves to His heart, which was very vigorous and uncorrupted, and thus tortured Him with incredible pain and suffering. And sometimes the pain shot from His heart to His lacerated members, and thus prolonged death with bitterness. And when my Son, surrounded with these pains, looked to His weeping friends—who would have preferred with His assistance to bear that penalty in their own persons, or to burn forever in Hell, rather than see Him thus tortured—this pain from the grief of His friends exceeded all bitterness and tribulation which He endured either in body or in heart, because He loved them tenderly. Then in His great anguish of body, He cried in His humanity to His Father: "Father, into Thy hands I commend My spirit." When I, His most afflicted Mother, heard these words, all my limbs trembled in my bitter grief of heart. And as often as I thought of this word, it was present and fresh in my ears. And as death came on, when His heart was breaking from excessive pain, then all His members quivered, and His head, rising slightly, inclined. His mouth was seen to open, disclosing His tongue all covered with blood. His hands shrunk a little from the holes of the nails, and the feet bore more of the weight of the body. His fingers and arms extended in a manner, and His back was pressed back on the cross. Then some said to me: "Mary, thy Son is dead." Others said: "He is dead, but He will rise again." While all were thus speaking, one came up and drove his lance so stoutly into His one side that it almost came out on the other; and when he drew out the lance, its point was all ruddy with blood. Then it seemed to me as if my heart was pierced, when I beheld the heart of my most beloved Son pierced through. Then He was taken down from the cross, and I received Him into my bosom, like a leper, and all livid, for His eyes were dead and full of blood, His mouth cold as snow, His beard like cords, His face contracted. His hands were so stiffened that they could not be raised above the navel. As He stood on the cross, so I held Him in my arms, like a man contracted in every limb. Then they swathed Him in clean linen, and I with my veil wiped His wounds and limbs, and I closed His eyes and mouth, which were open in death. They they laid Him in the sepulcher. Oh, how readily would I have laid myself there alive beside my Son, had it been His will! When all was over, John the good came and led me home. See, my daughter, what my Son endured for thee. (*Lib. i, c. 10*).

CHAPTER XVII

THE PASSION

When the Passion of my Son drew nigh, His eyes were filled with tears, and His body with sweat, through fear of the Passion, and He was soon torn from my sight; nor did I see Him more, till He was brought out to be scourged. Then He was dragged to the ground and dashed forward so cruelly that as His head struck, His teeth were dashed together, and He was so violently beaten on the neck and cheek that the sound of the blows reached my ears. Then at the lictor's order He stripped Himself of His clothes; voluntarily clasping the pillar, He was bound tightly, and His whole body lacerated with scourges tipped with sharp points turned back, not pulling out, but ploughing up. At the first blow, as if smitten in heart, I lost all sense; and coming to, after a time, I beheld His body torn, for He was all naked when He was scourged. Then one of His enemies said to the attending lictors: "Do you wish to put this man to death untried?" and saying this, he cut His bonds. And now my Son, loosed from the pillar, first turned to His clothes, but time was not given Him to dress. Yet as He was hurried along, He put His arms into the sleeves. But His footprints, where He stood at the pillar, were full of blood, so that I could easily discern every step He took by the bloody mark of the blood. Then with His tunic He wiped away the blood that streamed from His face.

When finally condemned, He was led out, bearing His cross; but on the way, another was put in His place to bear it. On reaching the place of the crucifixion, lo! the hammer and four sharp nails were ready, and at an order He laid off His clothes, bind-

ing around His loins a small linen cloth, which He
to His consolation received.

Now the cross was planted, and its arms raised, so
that the junction of the cross was between the
shoulders, the cross affording no support to the
head, and the inscription-board was fixed to the two
arms rising above the head. At an order given, He
turned His back to the cross, and being asked, first
stretched forth His right hand; then the other hand,
not reaching the other arm of the cross, was
stretched. And in like manner the feet were drawn to
the holes prepared for them and crossed. Parting
again below the knee, they were fastened to the
wood of the cross by two nails, as the hands were.

At the first blow of the hammer, I fell into an
ecstasy of grief, and on recovering, I beheld my Son
nailed to the cross, and I heard men saying to each
other: "What did He commit: theft, rapine, or false-
hood?" Others answering, [said] that He was a liar.
And then a crown of thorns was pressed tight on His
head, descending to the middle of His forehead,
many streams of blood flowing down His face from
the points that entered, filling His hair, and eyes,
and beard, so that He seemed to me nothing but
blood; nor could He see me standing by the cross except when He expelled the blood by compressing
His eyelids.

After commending me to His disciples, raising
His head, and lifting up His streaming eyes to

Heaven, He uttered a voice from the depth of His breast, saying: "My God, My God, why hast Thou forsaken Me?"—words that I could never forget till I came to Heaven, and which He uttered more through compassion for me, than affected by His own suffering. Then the color of death came on wherever He could be seen for the blood; His cheeks clung to His jaws, His attenuated ribs could be numbered; His belly, exhausted of all its humors, collapsed on His back, and His nostrils were pinched up, as His heart was almost broken. Then His whole body quivered, and His beard sank on His breast. Then I fell lifeless to the ground. His mouth being open, as He had expired, His tongue, teeth, and the blood in His mouth could be seen by those looking on, and His half-closed eyes were turned up; and His body, now dead, hung heavily, the knees inclining to one side, the feet to the other, on the nails as on hinges. Meanwhile, some men standing by said, as it were, exultingly: "Mary, thy Son is dead." Others of more sense said: "O lady, now the penalty of thy Son is paid to eternal glory." A short time after, His side being opened and the lance drawn out, the blood appeared on the spearhead, as it were, of a ruddy color, showing that the heart was pierced. This wound penetrated my heart, and it is wonderful that it did not burst. Others departed, but I could not.

But now I was consoled that I could touch His

body taken down from the cross, and receive Him to my bosom, examine His wounds, and wipe away the blood. Then my fingers closed His mouth, and I also composed His eyes; but I could not bend His stiffening arms so as to cross on His breast, but over His belly. Nor could His knees be extended, but they were bent as they had stiffened on the cross. *(Lib. iv, c. 70)*.

———•———

CHAPTER XVIII

THE CRUCIFIXION

St. Bridget Speaks

While I was at Mount Calvary weeping bitterly, I beheld my Lord, naked and scourged, led out by the Jews to be crucified, and diligently guarded by them. I then beheld, too, a hole cut in the mountain, and the crucifiers around, ready to perform their cruel work. But my Lord, turning to me, said to me: "Observe that in this hollow of the rock was the foot of My cross planted at the time of My Passion"; and I immediately saw how the cross was fixed there by the Jews, and fastened firmly in the hollow of the rock of the mountain, with wooden pegs driven in on all sides with mallets so that the cross should stand solidly and not fall. Now when the cross was firmly planted there, boards were set around the main piece of the cross like steps, as high up as where the feet of a crucified person would be, so that He and the crucifiers might ascend by these steps, and stand more conveniently on those boards to crucify Him. And after this they ascended those steps, leading Him with the greatest scoffing and insult. Joyfully ascending, like a gentle lamb led to the slaughter, when He was on those steps He extended His arm—not forced, but voluntarily—and opening His right hand, laid it upon the cross, which His cruel torturers barbarously crucified, driving the nail through the part where the bone was most solid. Then violently drawing His left hand with a rope, they affixed it to the cross in a similar manner. Then stretching His body beyond all bounds, they fastened His joined feet to the cross with two nails, and so violently extended those glorious limbs on the cross that all the nerves and veins were fairly broken. This done, they replaced on His head the crown of thorns, which they had taken off while affixing Him to the cross, and fastened it on His most sacred head. It so wounded His venerable head that His eyes were filled with the blood that flowed down. His ears, too, were closed, and His face and beard, as it were, covered and stained with that rosy blood.

His crucifiers and the soldiers immediately quickly removed all the boards placed up against the cross, and then the cross remained alone and lofty, and my Lord crucified upon it.

And when, full of grief, I beheld their cruelty, then I beheld His most dolorous Mother, as it were trembling and half dead—John and her sisters, who stood not far from the cross on the right, consoling her. The new pain of compassion for that most holy Mother so transfixed me that I felt as if a sharp sword of insupportable bitterness pierced my heart. At length, His dolorous Mother rising, as it were, lifeless in body, she looked on her Son, and stood thus supported by her sisters, overwhelmed with stupor, and, as it were, dead alive, pierced with a sword of grief.

When her Son beheld her and His friends weeping, He commended her in a mournful voice to John, and you might discern by His gesture and voice that from compassion for His Mother, His heart was pierced by the most keen dart of immense sorrow. Then His lovely and beautiful eyes took the hue of death; His mouth opened and appeared full of blood, His countenance pallid and sunken, livid and blood-stained; His body also was all livid and pallid, and very languid from the constant stream of flowing blood. The skin also, and virginal flesh of that most holy body, was so delicate and tender that a livid welt appeared from the slightest blow. Sometimes He endeavored to stretch Himself upon the cross, from the excessive bitterness of the intense and acute pain that He endured; for sometimes the pain from His members and pierced veins ascended to His heart and tortured Him cruelly with intense martyrdom, and thus His death was prolonged and dilated, with great torment and bitterness. Overcome by the excessive intensity of pain, and about to expire, He cried to His Father in a loud and mournful voice, saying: "O Father, why hast Thou forsaken Me?" Then His lips were pallid, and His tongue blood-stained, His belly collapsed and clinging to His back, as though He had no bowels within him. Again, then, He cried out in great grief and anguish: "Father, into Thy hands I commend My spirit"; and then His head was raised a little, then sank, and He gave up the ghost.

Then His Mother, seeing this, trembled all over, and would have fallen to the ground in her bitter anguish, had she not been supported by the other women. At that hour, His hands shrunk a little from the place of the piercing, in consequence of the great weight of His body, and it rested almost entirely on the nail with which the feet were attached to the cross. But His fingers and hands and arms were more extended than before; His shoulders and back were pressed on the cross.

Finally, all the Jews standing around, mockingly

cried against His Mother, saying many things; for some said: "Mary, thy Son is dead." Others spoke other jeering words, and thus, while the crowd stood around, one running up with great fury plunged a lance into His right side so powerfully that the lance seemed about to come forth in the opposite side of the body, and when it was drawn out, a very river of blood gushed impetuously from that wound; but the lance-head and part of the handle came forth blood-stained. His Mother, seeing this, trembled so violently and with bitter groans that her countenance and manner showed that her soul was then pierced with a keen sword of grief.

After this, when the crowd had departed, His friends took down Our Lord, whom His pious Mother received in her holy arms, and inclined Him, sitting on her knee, all wounded, torn, and livid; and then His dolorous Mother wiped His whole body and wounds with her veil, and closed His eyes, kissing them, and wrapped Him in a clean winding-sheet, and thus they bore Him, with great wailing and grief, and laid Him in the sepulcher. (*Lib. vii, c. 15*).

CHAPTER XIX

THE DEATH OF OUR LORD

The Blessed Virgin Speaks

At the death of my Son, all things were disturbed. For the divinity, which was never separated from Him, not even in death, in that hour of His death seemed to partake of His suffering, although the divinity could suffer no pain or penalty, being impassible and immutable.

My Son suffered pain in all His members and even in His heart, which nevertheless, being divine, is immortal; His soul, also, which was immortal, suffered because it left the body. The assembled angels also seemed to be, as it were, disturbed, when they saw God in humanity suffer on earth. But how could the angels, who are immortal, be troubled? Truly, like a just man, when he sees his friend suffer anything from which he is to reap great glory; he rejoices, indeed, for the glory he is to gain, but grieves, nevertheless, in a manner, for his suffering. So the angels grieved, as it were, for His Passion, although they are impassible. But they rejoiced at His future glory, and the benefit to result from His Passion. The elements, too, were all troubled; the sun and moon lost their splendor, the earth quaked, the rocks were rent, the graves opened, at the death of my Son.

All the Gentiles were troubled wherever they were, because there came in their hearts a certain sting of grief, although they knew not whence. The heart, too, of those who crucified Him, was in tribulation in that hour, but not for their glory. The very unclean spirits were troubled in that hour, and gathered together were troubled. Those, too, who were in Abraham's bosom, were much troubled, so that they would have preferred to be in Hell for eternity rather than behold their Lord paying such a penalty. But what pain I, who stood by my Son, a Virgin and His Mother, then suffered, no one can imagine. Therefore, my daughter, remember the Passion of my Son, fly the instability of the world, which is but a vision, and a flower that soon fadeth. (Lib. vi, c. 11).

CHAPTER XX

THE BURIAL OF OUR LORD

Daughter, thou shouldst think of five things: First, that all my Son's limbs were stiff and cold in death, and the blood which flowed from His wounds during His Passion adhered, coagulated, on all His

members. Second, that He was so bitterly and un-
mercifully afflicted in heart that it did not cease to
pain till the lance reached His side, and His heart,
divided, clung to the spear. Third, think how He was
taken down from the cross. The two men who took
Him down from the cross set up three ladders—one
reaching to His feet, another to His armpits and
arms, the third to the middle of His body. The first
ascended and held Him by the body; the second,
mounting another ladder, drew out first one of the
nails from one hand, then, changing the ladder, he
took out the nail from the other. These nails extended far beyond the wood of the cross. Then, he
who bore the weight of the body descending grad-
ually and moderately as he could, the other got up
the ladder reaching to the feet, and drew the nails
from the feet. And when he approached the ground,
one of them held the body by the head, and the other
by the feet, but I, being His Mother, held Him by
the middle. And so we three bore Him to a rock
which I had covered with a clean linen sheet, in
which we wrapped the body, but I did not sew the
winding-sheet. For I knew for certain that He would
not decay in the tomb. Afterwards, Mary Magdalen
and the other holy women came, and many holy
angels, like specks in the sunbeam, were present,
paying reverence to their Creator. What grief I then
felt, no one can tell. For I was like a woman in
childbirth, all of whose limbs after delivery are

tremulous, who, though she can scarcely breathe for pain, yet rejoices inwardly as much as she can, because she knows that her child is born never to return to the misery from which he came. So, though I was incomparably sad for the death of my Son, yet as my Son was to die no more, but live forever, I rejoiced in soul, and so a certain gladness was mingled with my grief. I can truly say that when my Son was buried, there were in a manner two hearts in one tomb. Is it not said: "Where thy treasure is, there is thy heart"? So my thoughts and my heart were ever in the sepulcher of my Son. *(Lib. ii, c. 21).*

----•----

CHAPTER XXI

OUR LADY'S COMPASSION

At the death of my Son, I was like a woman having her heart pierced with five lances. For the first lance was the shameful and opprobrious nudity, because I saw my most beloved and powerful Son standing naked at the pillar, and having no clothing. The second was His accusation, for they accused Him, calling Him a traitor and a liar, and even an assassin, whom I knew to be just and truthful, offending and wishing to offend no one. The third lance to me was the crown of thorns, which so cruelly pierced His sacred head that the blood flowed into His mouth, down His beard, and into His ears. The fourth was His piteous voice on the cross when He cried to His Father, saying: "O Father, why hast Thou forsaken Me?" as though He would say: "Father, there is none to pity Me but Thou." The fifth lance which pierced my heart was His most cruel death. My heart was pierced with as many lances as there were veins from which His precious blood gushed, for the veins of His hands and feet were pierced, and the pain of His lacerated nerves came inconsolably to His heart, and from His heart to the nerves again; and as His heart was most excellent and strong, as being formed of the best substance, therefore life and death contended, and thus life was bitterly prolonged in pain. But as death approached, when His heart was breaking with intolerable pain, then His limbs quivered, and His head, which had sunk on His shoulders, was slightly raised. His half-closed eyes were opened midway. His mouth, too, opened, and His tongue was seen drenched in blood. His fingers and arms, which were somewhat contracted, expanded. Having given up the ghost, His head sank on His breast, His hands sank a little from the place of the wounds; His feet sustained the greater weight. Then my hands dried up, my eyes were darkened, and my face became corpselike. My ears heard naught, naught could my mouth utter; my feet, too, shook, and my body fell to the earth. But rising from the ground, when I beheld my Son more fearful than a leper, I gave my will entirely to Him, knowing that all had been done according to His will, and that it could not have been done but by His permission, and I thanked Him for all. A certain joy was blended with my sorrow, for I beheld Him who never sinned, willingly, from His great charity, enduring such things for sinners. Let everyone, then, in the world, consider what I was at the death of my Son, and keep it ever before his eyes.

Consider the Passion of my Son, whose members were as my members, and as my heart. For He was within me as other children in their mother's womb; but He was conceived from the fervent charity of divine Love, others from the concupiscence of the flesh. Hence John, His cousin, says well: "The Word was made flesh," for by charity He came and abode in me, but the Word and charity formed Him in me. Hence He was to me as my heart. Hence, when He was born, I felt as though half my heart were born and went out of me. And when He suffered, I felt as though half my heart suffered, as when a body is half within and half without, when anything wounds what is without, that within feels it equally. So my heart was scourged and pierced when my Son was. I was nigher to Him in His Passion, and did not leave

Him. I stood nearer to His cross, and as what is nearer the heart wounds more keenly, so the pain of it was keener to me than to others. And when He looked upon me from the cross, and I on Him, then tears streamed from my eyes as from veins. And when He beheld me spent with grief, He was so afflicted by my pain that all the pain of His own wounds was, as it were, dulled at the sight of the grief in which He beheld me. Hence, I say boldly that His pains were mine, because His heart was mine. For as Adam and Eve sold the world for an apple, so my Son and I redeemed the world, as it were, with one heart. Think, then, how I was at the death of my Son, and you will not find it hard to leave the world. *(Lib. i, c. 27)*.

CHAPTER XXII

THE CONSIDERATION OF THE PASSION

The consideration of the Passion of my Son ought to be frequently in man's thoughts; for let him consider how the Son of God, the Son of the Virgin, who is one God with the Father and Holy Ghost, suffered; how He was led captive, and buffeted and spit upon; how He was scourged to the very inmost, so that the flesh was torn away by the lash; how with all His nerves distended and pierced, He stood dolorous on the cross; how, crying out on the cross, He gave up the ghost. If he frequently fans the spark, then will he grow warm. (*Lib. v, c. 20*).

FRUITS OF THE PASSION

Christ Speaks

I voluntarily gave Myself up to My enemies, and My friends remained, My mother in most bitter grief and pain. And though I saw the lance, nails, scourges, and other instruments of torture ready, I nevertheless went joyfully to My Passion. And although My head was bedewed with blood on all sides, and even if My enemies touched My very heart, I would rather have it divided than be deprived of thee. Thou art too ungrateful, then, if thou lovest Me not for so great charity. For if My head is pierced and bowed down on the cross for thee, thy head should be inclined to humility. And because My eyes were bloody and full of tears, so thy eyes should abstain from every delightful sight. And because My ears were full of blood, and heard words of detraction against Me, therefore let thy ears be turned away from scurrilous and foolish discourse. And as My mouth was filled with a most bitter draught, and cut off from good, so let thy mouth be closed to evil and open to good. And as My hands were extended with nails, by reason of thy works, which are signified by the hands, let them be extended to the poor and to My commandments. Let thy feet, that is, thy affections, by which thou shouldst go to Me, be crucified to pleasure, that as I suffered in all My members, so let them all be ready for My service. *(Lib. i, c. xi).*

HOW SINNERS CRUCIFY OUR LORD

Christ Speaks

I am God, who created all things for man's use, that they might all serve and edify man. But man abused, to his own destruction, everything that I created for his good. And what is more, he cares less for God, and loves Him less than he loves creatures. The Jews made Me undergo three kinds of torment in My Passion. First, the wood to which I was bound, scourged, and crowned. Second, the iron with which they pierced My hands and feet. Third, the draught of gall that they gave Me. Then they blasphemously called Me a fool, on account of the death which I freely met, and called Me a liar on account of My doctrine. Such are now multiplied in the world, and few give Me consolation. For they fasten Me to the wood by the will of sinning; they scourge Me by impatience, for no one can bear a single word for Me. They crown Me with the thorn of their pride, for they wish to be higher than I. They pierce My hands and feet with the iron of hardness, because they glory in sin, and harden their hearts so as not to fear Me. For gall they offer Me tribulation; for My Passion, to which I went joyfully, they call Me a liar and a fool. *(Lib. i, c. xxx).*

CHAPTER XXIII

LIFE OF THE BLESSED VIRGIN
AFTER OUR LORD'S ASCENSION

The Blessed Virgin Speaks

I lived a long time in the world after the Ascension of my Son; and God so willed it that many souls, seeing my patience and life, might be converted to Him, and the Apostles of God and other elect confirmed. And even the natural constitution of my body required that I should live longer, that my crown might be increased. For all the time that I lived, after the Ascension of my Son, I visited the

places in which He suffered and showed His wonders. So rooted, too, was His Passion in my heart,
that whether I ate or worked, it was ever as if fresh
in my memory. So, too, my senses were withdrawn
from earthly things, because I was only inflamed, as
it were, with new desires, and in turn, torn by grief.
Nevertheless, I so tempered my grief and joy that I
never omitted aught of God's services. And I so
dwelt among men as not to expect nor take even
aught of what is pleasing to man, except scanty food.
That my Assumption was not known to many nor
proclaimed by man, God, who is my Son, so willed,
that faith in His own Ascension should be first im-
planted in men's hearts, because the hearts of men
were hard and loth to believe His Ascension; how
much more would they have been so had my
Assumption been proclaimed in the very beginning
of the Faith. *(Lib. vi, c. 61)*.

Some years after the Ascension of my Son, I was
one day much afflicted with a longing to rejoin my
Son; then I beheld a radiant angel, such as I had
before seen, who said to me: "Thy Son, who is Our
Lord and God, sent me to announce to thee that the
time is at hand when thou shalt come bodily to Him,
to receive the crown prepared for thee." "Dost
thou," I replied, "know the day or hour when I shall
leave the world?" The angel answered: "The friends
of thy Son will come and inter thy body." Saying
this, the angel disappeared, and I prepared for my

departure, going, as was my wont, to all the spots where my Son had suffered; and when one day my mind was absorbed in admiring contemplation of divine charity, my soul was filled therein with such exultation that it could not contain itself, and in that very consideration, my soul was loosed from the body. But what magnificent things my soul then beheld; with what honor the Father, Son, and Holy Ghost then honored it, and by what a host of angels it was wafted up, thou canst not conceive, nor will I tell thee before thy soul and body are severed, although I have shown thee some of all these things in that prayer which my Son inspires thee. Those who lived with me when I gave up the ghost knew well, from the unusual light, that divine things then took place in me. After this, the friends of my Son, divinely sent, interred my body in the valley of Josaphat, countless angels, like specks in sunlight, attending, but malignant spirits not daring to approach. For fifteen days my body lay buried in the earth; then, with a multitude of angels, it was assumed into Heaven.

After my Son ascended to Heaven, I lived in the world fifteen years—the time from my Son's Ascension to my death. And when dead, I lay in the sepulcher three days; then I was taken up to Heaven with infinite honor and joy; but my garments in which I was interred, remained in the tomb, and I was then attired in such vesture as my Son and Lord,

Jesus Christ. Know, too, that there is no human body in Heaven but the glorious body of my Son and mine. *(Lib. vii, c. 26).*

---•---

CHAPTER XXIV

SELECT PRAYERS OF ST. BRIDGET

I

Almighty, everlasting God, who didst vouchsafe to be born for us of a most chaste Virgin, make us, we beseech Thee, serve Thee with a chaste body, and please Thee by a humble mind.

II

We pray thee, O most clement Virgin Mary, Queen of the world and of angels, to obtain relief for those whom the fire of Purgatory tries, pardon for sinners, perseverance in good for the just, and also defend us weak brethren from menacing danger. Through, etc.

III

O Lord, Holy Father, Who didst preserve intact in the tomb the body which Thou didst receive from the Virgin Mary for Thy Son, and didst raise it incorrupt, preserve, we beseech Thee, our bodies clean and immaculate in Thy most holy service, and direct our way in this time, that when the great and terrible day of judgment comes, they may be raised to life among Thy saints, and that our souls may eternally rejoice with Thee, and deserve to be associated with Thy elect.

IV

Blessed art thou, Mary, Mother of God, temple of Solomon, whose walls were golden, whose roof resplendent, whose pavement was laid with most precious stones; whose whole structure was splendid, its whole interior redolent and delightful to gaze upon. In every way art thou like to the temple of Solomon, in which the true Solomon walked and sat, unto which he brought in the ark of glory and the candlestick for light. So art thou, Blessed Virgin, the temple of that Solomon who made peace between God and man; who reconciled the guilty, who gave life to the dead, and delivered the poor from the executioner. For thy body and soul were made the temple of the Deity, wherein was the roof of divine charity, under which the Son of God, going forth from the Father to thee, dwelt joyfully with thee. The pavement of the temple was thy well-ordered life and assiduous exercise of virtues; for no grace was wanting in thee, for all in thee was stable, all humble, all devout, all perfect. The walls of the temple were square, for thou art troubled by no opprobrium, puffed up by no honor, disquieted by no impatience, seeking naught but God's love and honor. The pictures of thy temple were a constant fire of the Holy Ghost, whereby thy soul was so exalted that there was no virtue not more ample and perfect in thee than in any other creature. God walked in His temple when He infused into thy frame the sweetness of His visitation. He rested when the Deity was associated to the humanity. Blessed, therefore, art thou, O most Blessed Virgin, in whom the mighty God became a little child; the ancient Lord became a puny infant; the everlasting God and invisible Creator became a visible creature. Therefore, because thou art most compassionate and most powerful, O Lady, I beg thee to look on me and take pity on me. For thou art the mother of Solomon; not of him who was David's son, but of Him who is the Father of David, and the Lord of Solomon who built that wonderful temple which truly prefigured thee. For the son will hearken to the mother, and to such and so great a mother. Obtain, then, that the Infant Solomon who slumbered in thee may watch with me, so that no sinful delight sting me, that the contrition of my sins be permanent, love of the world be dead within me, my patience persevering, my penance fruitful. For I have no power for me, except one word, and that is:

"Mary, take pity!" For my temple is all the contrary of
thine; it is darkened with vices, soiled with luxury,
eaten by the worms of cupidity, unstable by pride,
tottering from the vanity of worldliness. *(Lib. iii, c.
29).*

V

Blessed art Thou, O my God, my Creator and
Redeemer. Thou art the ransom by which we have
been redeemed from captivity, by which we are
directed to all salutary things, by which we are associated to the Unity and Trinity. If I blush for my
own sloth, yet I rejoice that Thou who didst once die
for our salvation will die no more. For Thou art truly
He that was before the ages. Thou art He that has
power of life and death. Thou alone art good and
just. Thou alone art almighty and fearful. Blessed
then be Thou forever. But what shall I say of thee, O
Blessed Mary, the whole salvation of the world?
Thou art like pointing out suddenly to a friend
grieving for it, a lost jewel, whereby his pain is
alleviated, his joy increased, his whole mind
rekindled with joy. So thou, most sweet Mother,
didst show to the world its God, whom men had lost,
and didst bear Him in time who was begotten before
time, at whose birth earthly and heavenly things rejoiced. Therefore, O most sweet Mother, I beg thee
help me, lest the enemy rejoice over me or prevail
against me by his snares. *(Lib. iv, c. 75).*

CHAPTER XXV

PRAYERS ON THE PASSION OF OUR LORD

I

O Jesus Christ, eternal sweetness of them that hope in Thee, joy exceeding all joy and all desire, salvation, and love of sinners, who hast declared it to be Thy delight to be with the children of men, [Thou who wast] made man for man in the end of time; remember all Thy premeditation and interior grief which Thou didst endure in Thy human body at the approach of the time of Thy most saving Passion, preordained in Thy divine heart. Remember the sadness and the bitterness which, as Thou Thyself didst testify, Thou didst feel in Thy soul when at the Last Supper with Thy disciples Thou didst give them Thy Body and Blood, didst wash their feet, and sweetly consoling them, foretell Thy imminent Passion. Remember all the fear, anguish, and grief which Thou didst endure in Thy delicate body before the Passion of the cross when, after Thy thrice-repeated prayer and bloody sweat, Thou wast betrayed by Thy disciple Judas, taken by a chosen people, accused by false witnesses, unjustly judged by three judges, condemned innocent in the chosen city, at Paschal time, in the bloom of youth, stripped of Thy own clothing and clothed in the garments of another, buffeted, Thy face and eyes veiled, smitten with blows, bound to the pillar, scourged, crowned with thorns, struck with a reed on the head, and torn with numberless other acts of violence. Give me, O Lord God, I beseech Thee, before I die, in memory of these Thy passions before the cross, a true contrition, true confession, worthy satisfaction and remission of all my sins. Amen.

Our Father. Hail Mary.

II

O Jesus, Maker of the world, whom no measure by just bounds doth compass, who inclosest the earth in Thy palm, remember the most bitter grief which Thou didst endure when the Jews first fastened Thy most sacred hands to the cross with dull nails, and as Thou wast not agreeable to their will, added pain to pain in Thy wounds by perforating Thy most delicate feet, and cruelly wrenched and distended Thee the length and breadth of Thy cross, so that the joints of Thy limbs were loosened. I beseech Thee by the memory of this most sacred and bitter pain on the cross to give me Thy fear and love. Amen.

Our Father. Hail Mary.

III

O Jesus, heavenly physician, remember the languor, lividness, and pain which Thou didst suffer on the lofty scaffold of the cross, torn in all Thy limbs, not one of which had remained in its right state, so that no pain was found like to Thy pain; for from the sole of Thy foot to the top of Thy head there was no soundness in Thee. And yet, regardless of all pains, Thou didst piously pray to Thy Father for Thy enemies, saying: "Father, forgive them, they know not what they do." By this mercy and in remembrance of that pain, grant that this memory of Thy most bitter Passion be a full remission of all my sins. Amen.

Our Father. Hail Mary.

IV

O Jesus, true liberty of angels, paradise of delights, remember the grief and horror which Thou didst endure when all Thy enemies surrounded Thee like fierce lions, and tortured Thee by buffets, by spitting upon Thee, and by tearing and other unheard-of pains. By these pains and all the contumelious words and most severe torments whereby, O Lord Jesus Christ, all Thy enemies afflicted Thee, I beseech Thee to free me from all my enemies, visible and invisible, and grant me to reach the perfection of eternal salvation under the shadow of Thy wings. Amen.

Our Father. Hail Mary.

V

O Jesus, mirror of eternal brightness, remember the grief which Thou didst endure when Thou didst behold, in the mirror of Thy most serene Majesty, the predestination of the elect to be saved by the merits of Thy Passion, and the reprobation of the wicked to be damned by their own demerits; and by the abyss of Thy mercy, whereby Thou didst then compassionate us lost and hopeless sinners, and which Thou didst show the thief on the cross, saying, "This day thou shalt be with Me in Paradise," I beseech Thee, O merciful Jesus, show mercy on me at the hour of my death. Amen.

Our Father. Hail Mary.

VI

O Jesus, amiable King, and most desirable Friend, remember the sorrow Thou hadst when Thou didst hang naked and wretched on the cross, and all Thy friends and acquaintances stood over against Thee, and Thou didst find no comforter except alone Thy beloved Mother, most faithfully standing by Thee in bitterness of soul, whom Thou didst commend to Thy disciple, saying, "Woman, behold thy son." I beseech Thee, merciful Jesus, by the sword of grief which then pierced Thy soul, to have compassion on me in all my tribulations and afflictions, bodily and spiritual, and give me comfort in time of tribulation and at the hour of my death. Amen.

Our Father. Hail Mary.

VII

O Jesus, fountain of inexhaustible mercy, who from intense feeling didst exclaim on the cross, "I thirst," thirsting for the salvation of the human race, inflame, we beseech Thee, the desires of our hearts to every perfect work, and entirely cool and extinguish in us the thirst of carnal concupiscence and the heat of worldly delight. Amen.

Our Father. Hail Mary.

VIII

O Jesus, sweetness of hearts and great sweetness of minds, by the bitterness of the vinegar and gall which Thou didst taste for us, grant me at the hour of my death worthily to receive Thy Body and Blood, for the remedy and consolation of my soul. Amen.

Our Father. Hail Mary.

IX

O Jesus, royal virtue and mental delight, remember the anguish and pain which Thou didst endure when, from the bitterness of death and the reproaches of the Jews, Thou didst exclaim in a loud voice that Thou wast forsaken by Thy Father, saying, "My God, My God, why hast Thou forsaken Me?" By this anguish, I beseech Thee not to forsake me in my anguish, O Lord Our God. Amen.

Our Father. Hail Mary.

X

O Jesus, Alpha and Omega, ever virtue and life, remember that for us Thou didst plunge Thyself, from the top of Thy head to the sole of Thy feet, into the water of Thy Passion. By the length and breadth of Thy wounds, teach me, too much immersed in sin, to keep in true charity Thy broad command. Amen.

Our Father. Hail Mary.

XI

O Jesus, most profound abyss of mercy, I beseech Thee by the depth of Thy wounds, which pierced the marrow of Thy bones and vitals, raise me from the depth of sins in which I am plunged, and hide me in the hollow of Thy wounds, from the face of Thy wrath, till Thy anger pass away, O Lord. Amen.

Our Father. Hail Mary.

XII

O Jesus, mirror of truth, sign of unity, and bond of charity, remember the multitude of Thy innumerable wounds wherewith Thou wast wounded from the top of Thy head to the sole of Thy feet, and reddened with Thy most sacred Blood, which magnitude of pain Thou didst endure on Thy virginal flesh for us. O merciful Jesus, what more oughtest Thou do, and hast not done? Engrave, I beseech

Thee, O merciful Jesus, all Thy wounds in my heart
with Thy most precious Blood, that in them I may
read Thy sorrow and death, and in thanksgiving per-
severe duly to the end. Amen.

Our Father. Hail Mary.

XIII

O Jesus, most valiant Lion, immortal and uncon-
quered King, remember the pain which Thou didst
endure when all the powers of Thy heart and body
entirely failed Thee, and inclining Thy head, Thou
didst exclaim, "It is consummated." By that anguish
and pain, remember me in the last consummation of
my departure, when my soul shall be in anguish and
my spirit troubled. Amen.

Our Father. Hail Mary.

XIV

O Jesus, only-begotten Son of the most high
Father, splendor and figure of His substance,
remember the commendation wherewith Thou
didst commend Thy spirit to Thy Father, saying,
"Into Thy hands, O Lord, I commend My spirit";
and then, with lacerated body and broken heart,
with a loud cry, the bowels of Thy mercy exposed,
[Thou] didst expire to redeem us. By this precious
death I beseech Thee, O King of saints, strengthen
me to resist the devil, the world, flesh, and blood,
that dead to the world I may live to Thee; and in the

last hour of my departure receive Thou my exiled, wandering spirit returning to Thee. Amen.

Our Father. Hail Mary.

XV

O Jesus, true and fruitful vine, remember the overflowing and abundant effusion of blood which Thou didst pour forth in torrents, like wine pressed from the grape, when on the press of the cross Thou didst tread alone; and Thy side having been opened with a lance, Thou didst pour forth to us blood and water, so that not the least drop remained in Thee; and at last Thou wast suspended on high like a bundle of myrrh, and Thy delicate flesh fainted, and the moisture of Thy members dried up, and the marrow of Thy bones faded. By this most bitter Passion and the effusion of Thy precious Blood, O pious Jesus, I pray Thee, receive my soul in the agony of my death. Amen.

Our Father. Hail Mary.

O sweet Jesus, wound my heart, that tears of penitence and love may be my food night and day, and bring me entirely to Thee, that my heart may ever be habitable for Thee, and my conversation pleasing and acceptable to Thee; and the end of my life so praiseworthy, that after the close of this life, I may deserve to praise Thee with all Thy saints forever.

After five *Our Fathers* say the following prayer:

O Lord Jesus Christ, Son of the living God, receive this prayer in that most exceeding love wherewith Thou didst bear all the wounds of Thy most sacred Body, and remember me Thy servant, and to all sinners, and all the faithful, living and dead, give mercy, grace, remission, and eternal life. Amen.

THE END

If you have enjoyed this book, consider making your next selection from among the following . . .

Sermons of the Curé of Ars. *Vianney* 12.50
Revelations of St. Bridget of Sweden. *St. Bridget* 3.00
St. Catherine Labouré of the Miraculous Medal 13.50
The Glories of Mary. *St. Alphonsus* 10.00
St. Therese, The Little Flower. *Beevers* 6.00
Purgatory Explained. (pocket, unabr.) *Fr. Schouppe* 9.00
Prophecy for Today. *Edward Connor* 5.50
What Will Hell Be Like? *St. Alphonsus Liguori* .... .75
Saint Michael and the Angels. *Approved Sources* 7.00
Modern Saints—Their Lives & Faces. Book I. *Ball* 18.00
Our Lady of Fatima's Peace Plan from Heaven .... .75
Divine Favors Granted to St. Joseph. *Pere Binet* 5.00
Catechism of the Council of Trent. *McHugh/Callan* ... 24.00
Padre Pio—The Stigmatist. *Fr. Charles Carty* 15.00
Fatima—The Great Sign. *Francis Johnston* 8.00
The Incorruptibles. *Joan Carroll Cruz* 13.50
St. Anthony—The Wonder Worker of Padua. 5.00
The Holy Shroud & Four Visions. *Fr. O'Connell* 2.00
St. Martin de Porres. *Giuliana Cavallini* 12.50
The Secret of the Rosary. *St. Louis De Montfort* 3.00
Confession of a Roman Catholic. *Paul Whitcomb* 1.50
The Catholic Church Has the Answer. *Whitcomb* 1.50
True Devotion to Mary. *St. Louis De Montfort* 7.00
I Wait for You. *Sr. Josefa Menendez* .... .75
Words of Love. *Menendez, Betrone, etc.* 6.00
Little Lives of the Great Saints. *Murray* 18.00
Prayer—The Key to Salvation. *Fr. M. Müller.* 7.50
Sermons on Our Lady. *St. Francis de Sales* 10.00
Sermons of St. Alphonsus Liguori for Every Sun. 16.50
Alexandrina—The Agony and the Glory. 5.00
Life of Blessed Margaret of Castello. *Fr. W. Bonniwell* . 7.00
St. Francis of Paola. *Simi and Segreti.* 8.00
Bible History of the Old and New Tests. *Schuster* 10.00
Dialogue of St. Catherine of Siena 10.00
Dolorous Passion of Our Lord. *Emmerich* 16.50
Textual Concordance of the Holy Scriptures 35.00
Douay-Rheims Bible. *Leatherbound.* 35.00

—At your Bookdealer or direct from the Publisher.—
Call Toll-Free 1-800-437-5876.

Prices subject to change.